To:

Parker

From:

Grandpop +
Grandmom

Date:

02/14/16

DANIEL'S DIARY

How God Saved Me from the Lions

Allia Zobel Nolan

Illustrated by Linda Clearwater

HARVEST HOUSE PUBLISHERS

EUGENE, OREGON

Daniel's Diary

Text Copyright © 2009 by Allia Zobel Nolan
Art Copyright © 2009 by Linda Clearwater

Published by Harvest House Publishers
Eugene, Oregon 97402
www.harvesthousepublishers.com

ISBN 978-0-7369-2544-0

Original illustrations by Linda Clearwater. You may contact Linda at
lindaclearwater.com

Design and production by Mary pat Design, Westport, Connecticut

Printed in China

09 10 11 12 13 14 15 / LP / 10 9 8 7 6 5 4 3 2 1

For God, who always manages to send angels when I need them most; for my husband, Desmond, whose forbearance and love are my lifelines; for my mother, Lucille, for nurturing my love of reading and books, and for all my friends at Harvest House, who have been such "dreams" to work with.

Allia Zobel Nolan

To all of the friends who for many years have offered me their helping hands and hearts. They have pulled me from the pits of life on more occasions than I can count.

Linda Clearwater

Dear Friends,

"Wow," I said to myself when I first read the story of Daniel and the lions. "Daniel must have been really brave. His belief in God must have been really strong too." And all of that is certainly true.

But something else stuck in my mind about Daniel, and that is: He really knew how to pray.

See, Daniel never took prayer for granted. He thought of it as a great honor and privilege—and he made it a very important part of his day. He loved talking to God, thanking Him, and praising Him. And when he prayed, he always did it with respect—as though God were sitting right next to him.

That's a good picture for you and me to keep inside our heads when we pray. If we can imagine God right beside us, we'd be less likely to let our minds wander to silly things. We wouldn't rush through prayer because we were tired or hungry. And we'd be very sincere and pay close attention to what we were saying.

So, though we may never be able to show God how brave we are by spending the night in a lions' den, we can show Him how much we love Him by becoming experts at prayer, like Daniel. I'm going to try. How about you?

In the meantime, I hope you enjoy reading the adventures of Daniel; his friends Shadrach, Meshach, and Abednego; his royalness, King Darius; Scruffy the cat; and Louie the angel.

Blessings and joy.

Allia Zobel Nolan

Dear Diary,

Just when I think I'm through with this dream-reading stuff, some king or another calls for me, and it's "Daniel, can you tell me what this dream means?" and "Daniel, can you tell me what that dream means?" Oy veh. And you know Their Majesties can be very grumpy when they don't get the answers they want.

Belly's servant explains what the king saw.

Take, for instance, last night. My ex-boss's son, Belshazzar, (I called him Belly for short) sent his servant for me. Belly had a vision and wanted my advice.

"His Majesty has seen a hand... writing on the wall," Belly's servant told me as we walked to the palace.

"So?"

"So the hand wasn't connected to anything...you know, like a body. It was just five fingers," the servant replied, "writing on the wall."

"A party game of some sort, perhaps?" I asked the servant. "Or maybe His Majesty has had a little teeny tiny bit too much grape drink?"

The servant shrugged. "All I know is His Majesty said, 'Daniel will know what it means.'"

Mene—God has ended your reign,
Tekel—you're not doing a good job,
Parsin—your kingdom will be divided.

Come to find out, God was angry with Belly for praying to some statues and drinking wine from cups that belonged in God's house. So He sent him a message, three words written on the wall, and they weren't "I love you."

Naturally, I had to tell Belly the bad news, which boiled down to he wouldn't be His Highness for much longer. And by the end of the night, *poof!* Belly's enemy did away with him, and a new king by the name of Darius the Mede took over.

Actually, this turned out very good for me. Darius is a relative of a friend of mine. And today his servants came with the message that the king wants to see me about a job. I pray it has nothing to do with dreams.

Dear Diary,

Said my prayers, then off to the palace. My interview with the new king went well.

I met two men there, and it seems I'll be working with

Me, praying.

them. Not too friendly, though. Anyway, the new king gave us his plans on how he wants his government to run. Then, get this, he walks toward us with a huge sword. I'm thinking it might be time to run for it. But then he walks to the wall behind us and uses it to point to the map.

"My kingdom is far too big as it stands now," he says. "I need smaller, more manageable provinces."

Then, with a flick of his wrist, he slices and dices the map into puzzle piece bits.

"Now," he says, "that's better. There are 120 provinces, and I shall put a governor in command of each. Then you three will be in charge of the governors. You'll handle all the paperwork and

Darius, cutting up his map into 120 pieces

report to me. Less work for mother," he says. "Understand?"

We all nodded our heads and said, "Yes, Sire, Your Grace, may you live forever."

"Good," he answered. "That's settled. Let's eat!"

So in walk servants with all sorts of food: leg of lamb, tongue of cow, oxtail stew, chicken fricassee, fish and chips, you name it. But, of course, nothing I could eat.

"What's the matter, Danny? On a diet?" the king asked.

"Sorry, Your Graciousness, may you live forever, but I'm veggie," I said, and then I cringed as I waited for an angry reply.

"No problem-o," the king said, matter of factly. "Chef makes a mean cheese omelet."

And, Diary, you'll never guess. It was the best cheese omelet I ever ate. I think I'm going to like this job.

Dear Diary,

Had a working breakfast with the king today. Here's what happened.

"May you live forever!" I said when I saw him. Then I noticed he wasn't alone. He had a Persian cat in his lap, and he was petting her as he talked.

"Enough with the live forever stuff," the king said. "You've come highly recommended, Danny. So sit down and tell me all about yourself." Then he said to the cat, "Say hello to the nice man, Scruffy." And right on cue, the cat came over and gave me a head butt.

"She likes you," the king said, overjoyed. "Scruffy likes you. She doesn't like everyone, you know. You should take that as a great compliment."

"Oh, for sure, Your Royalness," I said as I scratched Scruffy under her chin.

"Come back to Daddy now," the king said to his pet, and, of course, she did. Then he started talking baby talk to her and combing her long coat.

Scruffy giving me a head butt.

"Ahem," I said, and the king motioned for me to tell my story.

"Well, as you know I'm a Hebrew, a dream reader, and I studied three years under King Nebuchadnezzar, after he sacked Jerusalem.

"Now Uncle Nebby (I called him Uncle Nebby) ate a lot of spicy food," I told the king. "So he had a lot of bad dreams. And this one time, you may have heard about it, he had a dream, but didn't want anyone to interpret the dream. Instead, he wanted someone to tell him WHAT he dreamt. When no one could, he got angry and threatened to put all his advisors to death, including me.

DANIEL
1. Dream Reader
2. Hebrew
3. Studied under King Nebby

Me, explaining me.

I asked for an extension, and my friends and I prayed to God. God heard us and told me exactly what my uncle had dreamt.

"Needless to say, Uncle Nebby was thrilled. 'Your God is awesome,' he said to me. 'He is the Lord of lords, and the revealer of mysteries. We must all praise Him.'

"And that's what we did. So no one's throat was cut, and I actually got a raise.

More...

"But Uncle Nebby had a short memory," I continued. "And before you could turn around twice and touch your nose, he had built a huge idol—90 feet high and 9 feet wide—and insisted that everybody bow down to it.

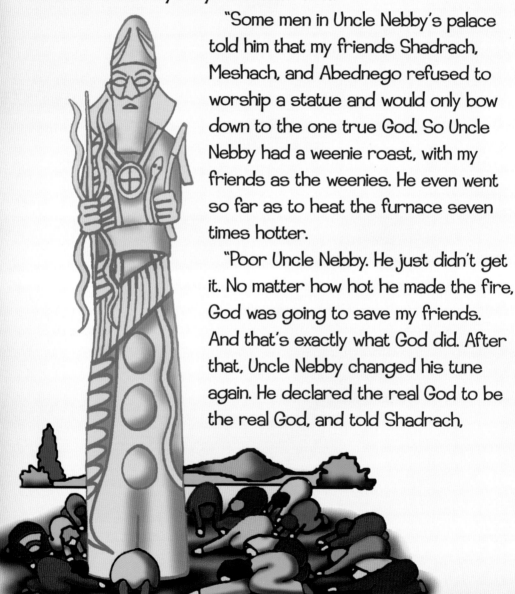

"Some men in Uncle Nebby's palace told him that my friends Shadrach, Meshach, and Abednego refused to worship a statue and would only bow down to the one true God. So Uncle Nebby had a weenie roast, with my friends as the weenies. He even went so far as to heat the furnace seven times hotter.

"Poor Uncle Nebby. He just didn't get it. No matter how hot he made the fire, God was going to save my friends. And that's exactly what God did. After that, Uncle Nebby changed his tune again. He declared the real God to be the real God, and told Shadrach,

Meshach, and Abednego to freshen up, after which he praised their bravery and promoted them.

Shadrach, Meshach, and Abednego coming out of the fire.

"When Uncle Nebby died, I did a bit of dream reading for Belly, your predecessor, which brings us to the present date, and you, Your Royalness, may you live forever."

"Well, I hope you're as good with government administration as you are with dreams," the king said to me.

"Actually, I got high honors in Abacus, Motivational Skills, and Handling Small Provinces on Ten Drachmas a Day," I told him. "True dream readings come from God, but don't worry, Great King. God and I are tight."

My wall of fame.

"Well, Danny," the king said, "don't disappoint me. Care to stay for dinner? We're having poached pigeon, Scruffy's favorite," he said. "Cook can make you brussel sprouts. Oh, and, Danny, can you play Go Fish?"

"None better," I said. "I'll be back after evening prayers, Your Honorableness."

You know, Diary, he's not a bad boss, this Darius.

Dear Diary,

Don't know if I told you, but my position comes with a place to live. I have great wide windows that look toward Jerusalem, which reminds me, it's time for prayers. I must thank God for all these great blessings. Back in a half hour.

Okay, Diary. I'm back. Where was I? Oh, yes, it's nice here. The king and his cat have turned out to be friendly, and I'm enjoying my new job very much.

I'm working like a demon—no, scratch that—I'm working like a beaver, and things are going well.

My satraps are shaping up, and my seminar on Building Better Relationships with Slaves and Other

At the office, working.

Foreign Employees was a big hit. My Vice President of Collecting Taxes is, praise the Lord, honest. And, thank God, those who report directly to me are loyal and hardworking. I gave them an extra day off for Passover. The king thought it was good for team building.

My coworkers, Aaron and Ezra, are still a problem, though. No matter what I do they ignore me; that is, when they're not in a corner whispering and pointing at me. I can't remember saying or doing anything to offend them. All I can think of is that they must be jealous.

I try to be helpful. Why, just last week when both governors had problems in their provinces, I offered them a private session of my Managing Small Provinces seminar for free.

"We could go to Falafel Joe's for dinner, afterward—my treat," I suggested.

But all I got was a cold shoulder.

Oh, well, like I said, at least my boss is nice. Can't have everything.

My coworkers, Aaron and Ezra, whispering about me.

Dear Diary,

We had our six-month review at the palace today. The king brought all three of us into a room with maps, pull-down charts, and scrolls of statistics. Nobody realized, but he had been keeping close tabs on us all the while.

"You know, Danny," he said to me, pointing to some numbers on the chart, "you really are doing a great job. Not like these twits over here."

"Ah, thank you, Your Greatness," I answered. "But, Your Wonderfulness," I continued, trying to put in a good word, "my fellow governors would have done the same had it not been for a string of bad luck."

"Nice try, Danny," replied the king, "but these freeloaders need to get with the program—spend less time at the camel races and more time at the office. And they'd better do it fast if they want to hold onto their heads."

"Yes, Sire, Your Exaltedness," Ezra and Aaron said. They were shaking in their sandals.

"Now," said the king, walking back and forth. "I called you all here because I'm changing the chain of command. I'm making Danny Boy my Number One Man, the

Ezra and Aaron giving me their pay. Boy, were they mad!

Big Cheese, the Head Honcho (next to me, that is). You two will report directly to him—not me—from now on. Oh, and you both get a pay cut so I can give Danny a raise. Is that clear?"

"Yes, Your Greatness," the two governors said, staring daggers at me.

"Now, you two, take a hike," the king ordered. "And Danny, let's play Go Fish."

Playing cards with Darius. I let him win...

Needless to say, Ezra and Aaron were NOT happy. They left in a huff, but not without threatening me under their breaths. They called me a cheater and told me to "watch my back." I'm hoping this will blow over. But I'm feeling trouble in my bones.

Dear Diary,

Things are great, and the king came through with my promotion. Most folks are happy for me, except, of course, Aaron and Ezra. One of my executive vice presidents said he heard them questioning workers about my habits.

Was I fair? they wanted to know. Did I tell too many bad jokes, bet on the camels, wear polyester prayer shawls? Did I have my hand in the cookie jar? Stuff like that. But every employee they asked had a good word for me.

Which reminds me, time to pray. Back at you later.

Well, I just got word about what Aaron and Ezra are up to. They know I pray to the Lord three times a day, and that nothing would stop me, ever. So they came up with a cockamamy new law about prayer.

See, Darius worships these gold statues he has in the palace. He thinks they helped him conquer Babylon. And as

Belly and Scruffy worshiping a gold false god statue.

king, he actually believes he's the *son* of these false gods. Go figure. Now I tried to tell him about the real, true God, how there is only one and it's the Lord. But Darius can be kind of stubborn sometimes. And I didn't push it.

So Aaron and Ezra went to Darius and whispered in his ear. "You are the divine son of the gods," they said, making him feel really good about himself.

"As such, why not have a pray-a-thon to you, O Awesome King? Let's just say that for one entire month you get the lion's share of worship," they said. "That means everyone has to pray to you and only you. Surely, you deserve it, O Great King. Don't you think? Huh? What do you say?"

"Well, now," King Darius said, beaming. "You guys have finally come up with an idea that isn't half-baked, for a change. What do you think, Scruffy? Should everybody pray to Daddy for a month?"

Darius signing Ezra and Aaron's new law.

Of course, the cat meowed, and Darius signed the law.

I heard it was a long, involved decree, with lots of "to wits," "parties of the first person," and "parties of the second persons," and something about a lions' den in it. I'll find out more tomorrow.

Dear Diary,

It's day one of the new law, and things have been quiet.

So I'm going to work as usual, and I'll be home at noon for my prayers. Oh, and the penalty for breaking this new law? You get fed to the lions. But Darius is my friend, and I'm his right-hand man. I doubt very much the new rule will apply to me.

Catch you later.

Guards putting up a sign.

Well, I spoke too soon. Things have certainly heated up. Those two tattletales caught me praying today and God only knows what will happen.

"Aha!" both of them screamed when they saw me kneeling.

They almost gave me a heart attack. "You're worshipping your God, aren't you?" they yelled.

"Well, I'm not looking for dust bunnies," I told them.

"Aha!" they said again. "You admit it."

Me, saying (what else?) my prayers.

"Of course. I pray three times every day. And both of you know it, don't you?"

"We'll ask the questions here," they snapped, and then they stuck their fingers in my face. "Are you not aware that the new law prohibits praying to anyone but His Most Highness, Dairus the King, for 30 days...or else...?"

"I'm aware," I replied. "But I don't pray to men. I pray to God. So, if you'll excuse me..." And with that they seized me and took me to the king.

"Daniel was caught praying to his God, Your Most Graciouness," Ezra told Darius. Then Aaron chimed in, "Yes, he broke the law. And I quote article 75, section IV, which states there are no exceptions, 'not for friends, relatives, pets, mother-in-laws, or insects.' You signed it. Now you have to do what you said you would."

"Well, Danny Boy, is it true?" The king stared at me. There were tears in his eyes.

More...

Just then, Scruffy, the king's cat, walked over and brushed up against my leg. When the guard tried to shoo her away, she hissed and scratched his hand.

"May you live forever, King Darius," I answered. "You know I pray to God every day. You know I can't do otherwise."

"Well, Danny, this puts me in an awkward position. Persian laws don't have loopholes, you know. And once I sign a decree, I can't undo it." Then the king picked up the cat and paced back and forth, carrying her.

"Oh, this is very bad," he muttered. "Very bad. But a law is a law, Danny, and I'm going to have to do something I don't want to do: throw you in the lions' den."

Ezra jumping up and down about my going to the lions' den.

"OH, GOODY, GOODY, GOODY!" shouted Ezra, clapping his hands with glee. When he realized what he had done, though, he wiped the smile off his face and turned serious. "What I mean is, how awful for you, Danny Boy," he said and then repeated, "but you know, a law is a law."

Dairus looked pale. So I took him by the arm and said, "Listen, Your Wonderfulness. Don't worry. You do what you have to. I'm sure God will take care of me. I'm not afraid. Of course, I've never *had* a sleepover with the lions, but hey, I like cats. They like me. So let me just get some pajamas. I'll be ready in a half hour."

"Danny, you know I don't want to do this," the king said, sadly. "There's no one in the whole kingdom who plays Go Fish like you, and Scruffy will miss you too. But..."

"It's okay, My King," I said. "No problem-o." And then I left to get my things.

Me, telling Darius and Scruffy "God will protect me."

Dear Diary,

Guards are waiting outside, so I have to be quick. The plan is to march me over to the lions' den and throw me in. On top of that, Ezra and Aaron insisted the king put his seal on the heavy rock-in case I try to get out. As if. Boy, do they have it in for me!

Writing in my diary before guards take me away.

I know God will do what He thinks is right. But I AM a teeny bit nervous. I've walked by that pit dozens of times and heard lots of GURGLINGS from the lions' empty stomachs. The poor things only get fed once a month, if they're lucky.

Still, God has always looked out for me. And look at Shadrach, Meshach, and Abednego. God saved them from the fiery furnace, didn't He? I just have to have faith and be brave. Whatever happens, God is great!

Catch you later...

It's early morning now. AND YES, I'M STILL HERE! AND OH WHAT A NIGHT!!! HAVE I GOT SOME NEWS FOR YOU!!!

Well, the king, his cat, Ezra, Aaron, and some soldiers watched as two guards threw me into the pit. "Maybe your God will save you, Danny," the king called after me. "Ah...that is, I'm sure your God will save you. And thanks for being a good sport about this."

"No worries, Your Awesomeness," I yelled back. So, now, here I am in this pitch-black pit, trying to adjust my eyes to the darkness. It was almost eleven o'clock, and the lionesses and their cubs were sleeping. So I tiptoed to a corner, when, suddenly, a lion as big as two water buffalos let out an earsplitting ROOOOARRRRRR! He was just about to pounce on me, when I said, through chattering teeth...

One very nervous me, trying to calm one very large lion.

"Hi, there. I'm Daniel, and I'm really sorry to drop in like this. I know it's late, but the king signed this law and, well, here I am. I won't hurt you. Why not just go back to sleep while I kneel down here in the corner and pray?"

So that's what I did. The lion cocked his head and watched me.

More...

"Lord," I prayed. "You know I love You with all my heart, and I have faith You'll do the right thing. But, if You are planning to save me, may I suggest You do it in the next five minutes?"

When I opened my eyes, the lion was still there, only now he had a bib on and eight friends with him. It was probably my imagination, but I thought I heard them chanting, "Yum, yum, yummy, yum, yum."

Then, suddenly, SWHOOSH! in flies this really tall angel and stands between me and the lions. Even in his robe, I could see this was no ordinary angel. He had muscles everywhere. He looked like a poster for Mr. Olympia.

Louie, the angel, arrives just in time.

"Sorry I'm late. Got held up on another job for God," the angel said.

"Well, actually, I was just in the middle of praying. Give me half a minute, will you?"

"You betcha," the angel said.

"And, Lord, thank You so much for sending me this wonderful angel...ah...what's your name?"

"Louie."

"Lord, thanks so much for sending me Louie. I knew You'd save me. For these and all the many blessings You give me, I praise Your name. Amen.

"So, ah, Louie," I asked the angel, "what's the plan?"

"Well, actually, Daniel," Louie said, "God told me to close the lions' mouths." And before you could say, "Dinner isn't served," Louie went around and did just that. I have to admit it-it looked pretty funny.

"Now listen up," Louie the angel said to the lions. "This is just temporary. You'll be back to normal tomorrow at noon. It's just that Daniel here is a good friend of God's, and God doesn't want anything to happen to him. *Comprende?*"

Louie, lecturing the lions and shutting their mouths.

All the lions nodded their heads up and down. And with that, Louie the angel and his muscles were gone.

More...

After that, I walked over to a rock and sat down.

The lions were all looking at me. So I said, "Look, I know this isn't the most comfortable thing for you guys. But it's all for the glory of God. God wants us to have faith in Him. And even when we're afraid, or in your case, up tight, we should turn to Him and never give up praying to Him."

Then I said, "It will be dawn in a little while. Why don't I tell you the story of my friends Shadrach, Meshach, and Abednego..."

So I did, and before long, they were all asleep.

Then I fell asleep.

Okay, so morning arrived, and I'm kind of dozing; the lions are just waking up and stretching, when I hear this yelling:

"Danny? Danny, my boy? Are you all right? Has your God saved you?" It's the king.

28

Well, I love Darius to death, but I couldn't resist having some fun, so I called out...

"My Great King, may you live forever. Yes, the Lord God has saved me, but there was a little mix-up and I'm speaking to you from the belly of a lion. Do you think you can get me out? It's a bit dark in here."

"Ohmygoodness," I heard the king say. "Hold on, Danny Boy. Guards! Don't just stand there!"

I make King Darius think I'm in the belly of a lion.

So the guards rolled back the stone, and there I stood smiling and waving.

"Just kidding, My King," I said, climbing out of the pit. "God sent an angel last night to shut the lions' mouths. I had faith He'd save me, and He did."

"Danny, I can't tell you how happy I am to see you. I was a nervous wreck all night."

Darius and Scruffy are really happy to see me.

Even more...

The king rushed past the guards, and gave me a big hug. Since he was carrying Scruffy, the poor cat almost got squished.

Then the king put his arm around me and walked me back to the palace.

"You must tell me everything," he said, "but first let's eat. I'm famished. Some steak for me, broccoli quiche for you, and lots of hot coffee. I didn't sleep a wink."

"Yes, Your Gracefulness," I answered. "But I hope you don't mind if I get out of my pajamas, freshen up a bit, and say my prayers first."

"You go ahead, Danny Boy. There's some business I have to attend to," the king said. As I walked off I heard the king ordering Ezra and Aaron to inspect the lions' den and have a full report on his desk by the morning. I hope they finish before noon.

Anyway, at lunch I told the king the whole story—about the lions, how God saved me, and, of course, about Louie the angel. "He had biceps like watermelons."

"You know, Danny," the king said after we'd had our fill. "I think this calls for a new law."

Uh-oh. Ezra and Aaron go to inspect the den just as the lions' mouths are opened.

So he sat down, pulled out a quill, and wrote a decree. "Be it known that in all provinces of my kingdom, all people will, from now on, honor and respect one God, the true God, Daniel's God."

After that, we played six games of Go Fish with Scruffy looking on. And, as usual, I let my friend Darius win.

King Darius signs the law. Then it's time for Go Fish. Guess who wins?

THE END

GLOSSARY

A

administration—the business of running or taking care of something, like an office, country, or in this case, a province

C

cold shoulder—to be unfriendly to someone, ignore, or not include them in anything

cockamamy—silly, wacky, unbelievable, something that does not make sense or is ridiculous

D

drachmas—a name used for a kind of money in Bible times

demon—a bad or evil spirit; fallen angel

decree—another name for a law

F

faith—being sure about something; believing in God and what He says

I

idol—a statue made of stone or gold which people prayed to instead of praying to God, or anything people make more important than God in their lives

interpret—to explain what something means

L

lion's share—the biggest share of something

P

predecessor—someone who did something before the person who is doing it now

province—a part of a county

S

satraps—another name for a Persian governor

scroll—in Bible times, a roll of paper people used to write on

V

vision—an image or picture people see in their minds. God sometimes uses visions to communicate, explain, or show something to people

W

worship—praying to, singing, or praising God

Daniel answered…
"My God sent his angel,
and he shut the
mouths of the lions.
They have not hurt me."

Daniel 6:21-22